topps
MATCH ATTAX

2019

MANCHESTER CITY

Manchester City stormed to Premier League triumph in 2018! They won a record 18 games in a row to lift their third league trophy in just six years.

TACTICS TALK

Manchester City only let in 27 goals and scored an amazing 106 in 2017-18. Manager Pep Guardiola's plan was to press the opposition in numbers and win the ball, before unleashing players like Kevin De Bruyne, Leroy Sane and Raheem Sterling in lightning-quick attacks. Defenders Kyle Walker and Fabian Delph raced down the wings to cross and set up strikers Sergio Aguero and Gabriel Jesus, who scored 34 goals between them.

3 SICK STARS

DAVID SILVA The little Spaniard bossed Manchester City's midfield, scoring an impressive nine Premier League goals and 11 assists.

EDERSON The keeper cost a mega £35 million in 2017, but he was worth every penny, keeping 16 clean sheets in the league.

RAHEEM STERLING Playing on the right, left or in the middle, the England midfielder was absolutely epic and grabbed 18 Premier League goals.

PAST HERO

GEORGI KINKLADZE

The tricky midfielder was a sensational Manchester City hero between 1995 and 1998. He scored wonder goals and dribbled past defenders as if they were statues. Kinkladze even turned down Barcelona to stay at the club!

STAR TO WATCH IN 2019

PHIL FODEN

The 18-year-old won the Under-17 World Cup with England in 2017 and this could be the season he really makes his mark in the Premier League. An exciting midfielder who loves to score and create goals – watch out for this left-footed ace ripping it up!

Time for some weightlifting practice.

SEASON STATS

POSITION: 1ST
PREMIER LEAGUE POINTS: 100
PREMIER LEAGUE WINS: 32
PREMIER LEAGUE GOALS SCORED: 106
QUICKEST GOAL SCORED: 39 SECONDS (STERLING VERSUS WATFORD)
QUICKEST GOAL CONCEDED: 9 MINUTES (VERSUS LIVERPOOL FC)
YELLOW/RED CARDS: 59/2
FIRST TEAM PLAYERS USED: 27

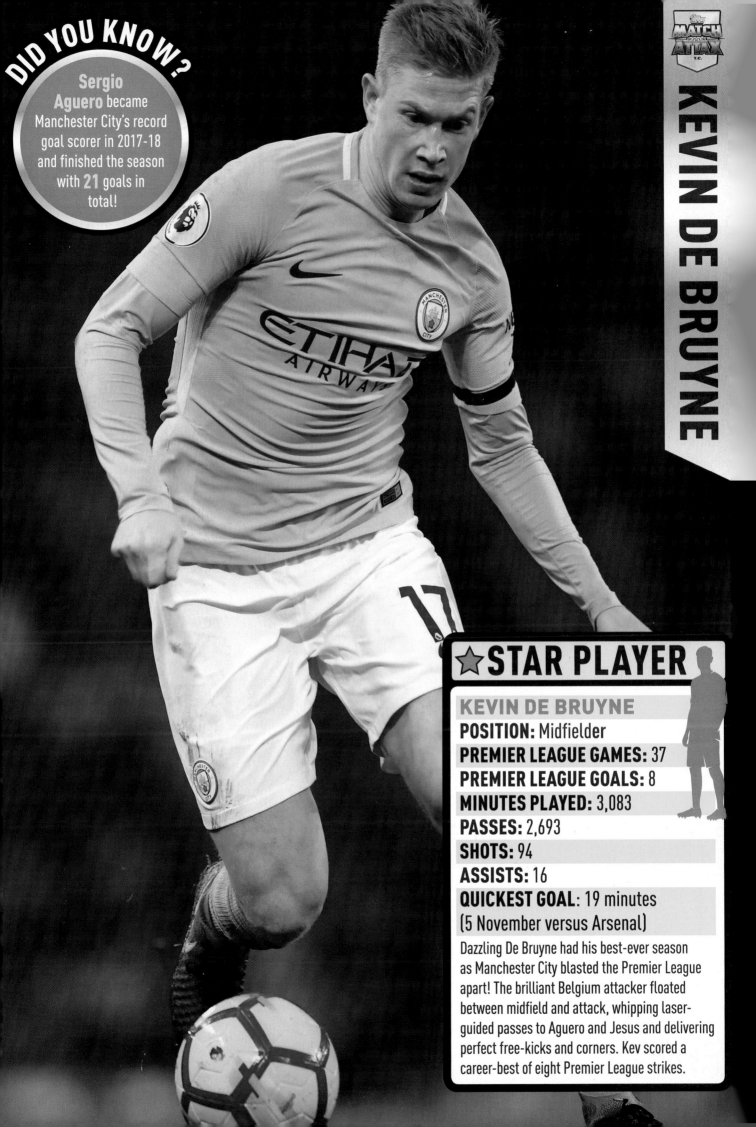

KEVIN DE BRUYNE

⭐ STAR PLAYER

KEVIN DE BRUYNE

POSITION: Midfielder

PREMIER LEAGUE GAMES: 37

PREMIER LEAGUE GOALS: 8

MINUTES PLAYED: 3,083

PASSES: 2,693

SHOTS: 94

ASSISTS: 16

QUICKEST GOAL: 19 minutes (5 November versus Arsenal)

Dazzling De Bruyne had his best-ever season as Manchester City blasted the Premier League apart! The brilliant Belgium attacker floated between midfield and attack, whipping laser-guided passes to Aguero and Jesus and delivering perfect free-kicks and corners. Kev scored a career-best of eight Premier League strikes.

MANCHESTER UNITED

In 2018, The Red Devils secured their highest league finish since 2013. Jose Mourinho's men look much more like the club's famous title-winning teams of the past!

TACTICS TALK

Manchester United scored fewer goals than rivals Manchester City and Liverpool FC, but they picked up an impressive 25 wins to finish second. With a solid defence, featuring Phil Jones, Chris Smalling and Antonio Valencia, Mourinho's creative force ahead of them included Juan Mata, Jesse Lindgard and Paul Pogba. Romelu Lukaku was the striking spearhead, with Marcus Rashford and Anthony Martial hitting the net, too.

3 SICK STARS

DAVID DE GEA In 2018 De Gea proved what a world-class goalkeeper he is with a string of superhero saves and top displays.

PAUL POGBA The Frenchman can score, tackle, pass and assist. His double at Manchester City was a highlight for him.

ANTHONY MARTIAL Despite not always starting, the speedy forward still managed to strike double figures in goals during the season.

PAST HERO
RYAN GIGGS

Oops! Handball!

With a club record of 963 appearances between 1991 and 2014, midfielder Ryan Giggs is a real legend at Old Trafford. The Welshman won 13 Premier League titles and two UEFA Champions League medals and was also caretaker manager at the end of his playing career with the club.

STAR TO WATCH IN 2019
ALEXIS SANCHEZ

After joining from Arsenal in January 2018, Sanchez took a while to settle at Manchester United. But he's ready to once again show all of his skills and penalty box powers at Old Trafford – when Sanchez bursts into the area defenders need to keep a very close eye!

SEASON STATS

POSITION: 2ND
PREMIER LEAGUE POINTS: 81
PREMIER LEAGUE WINS: 25
PREMIER LEAGUE GOALS SCORED: 68
QUICKEST GOAL SCORED: 11 SECONDS (ERIKSEN VERSUS MANCHESTER UNITED)
QUICKEST GOAL CONCEDED: 3 MINUTES (VERSUS BURNLEY)
YELLOW/RED CARDS: 64/1
FIRST TEAM PLAYERS USED: 27

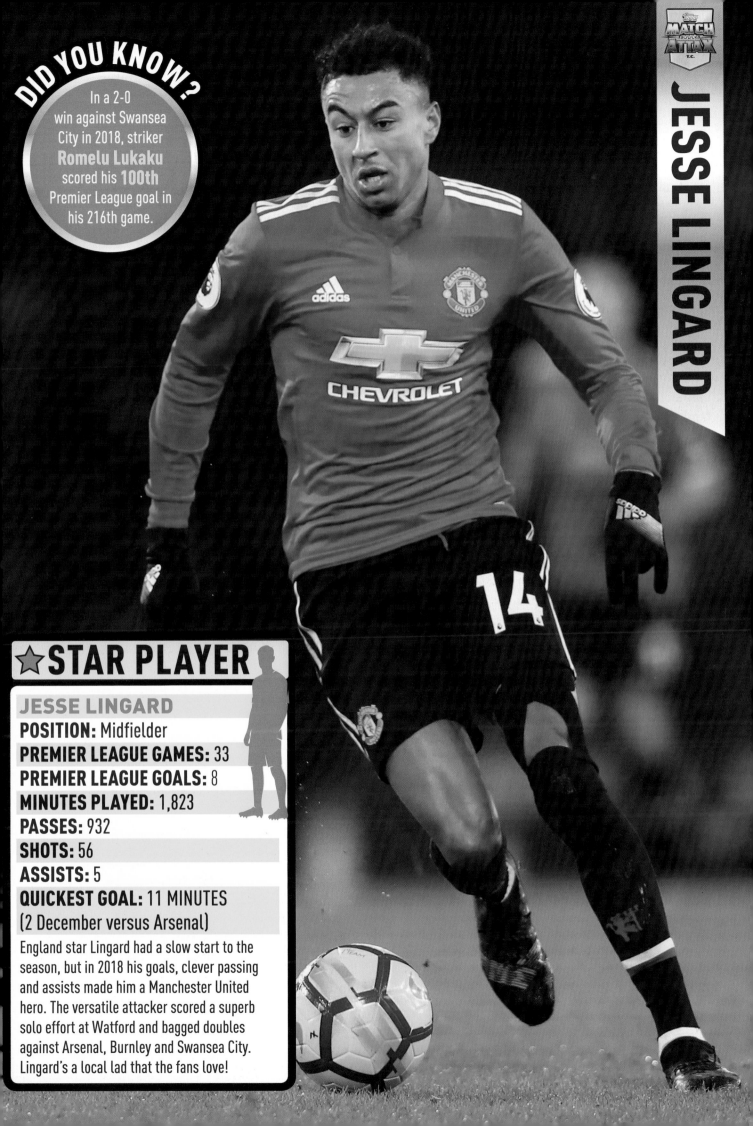

DID YOU KNOW?

In a 2-0 win against Swansea City in 2018, striker **Romelu Lukaku** scored his **100th** Premier League goal in his 216th game.

⭐ STAR PLAYER

JESSE LINGARD

POSITION: Midfielder
PREMIER LEAGUE GAMES: 33
PREMIER LEAGUE GOALS: 8
MINUTES PLAYED: 1,823
PASSES: 932
SHOTS: 56
ASSISTS: 5
QUICKEST GOAL: 11 MINUTES (2 December versus Arsenal)

England star Lingard had a slow start to the season, but in 2018 his goals, clever passing and assists made him a Manchester United hero. The versatile attacker scored a superb solo effort at Watford and bagged doubles against Arsenal, Burnley and Swansea City. Lingard's a local lad that the fans love!

TOTTENHAM HOTSPUR

Spurs fans had more memorable moments to enjoy in 2018. Here's all the London club's top stats and stars, plus the footy facts you need to know!

TACTICS TALK

With three top-four Premier League finishes in a row, manager Mauricio Pochettino has turned Tottenham Hotspur into one of the fiercest teams in the country. With Harry Kane up front, the team usually sets up in a 4-2-3-1 formation. Two holding midfielders play behind a forward trio of Son, Alli and Eriksen, with full-backs Trippier and Davies working hard out wide.

STAR TO WATCH IN 2019

LUCAS MOURA

The winger moved to Tottenham Hotspur in January after a £25 million switch from PSG. The exciting Brazilian took time to settle at the club, but he's ready to show the fans what a devastating mix of pace and power he has. His right foot can light up Spurs' attacks!

3 SICK STARS

HEUNG-MIN SON With his right foot, left foot or head, Son scores all sorts of crucial goals for Tottenham. He links up superbly with Kane.

JAN VERTONGHEN The experienced centre-back keeps Spurs' backline strong and uses his positional sense to cut out danger.

DELE ALLI Using his slick skills, speed, passing and quality shooting, Alli always does the business from his attacking midfield spot.

PAST HERO GLENN HODDLE

One of the most stylish midfielders Spurs have ever produced, Glenn Hoddle starred for the club between 1975 and 1987. He made 377 league appearances, scored 88 goals and won the FA Cup and UEFA Cup. Hoddle also managed Spurs from 2001 to 2003.

SEASON STATS

POSITION:	3RD
PREMIER LEAGUE POINTS:	77
PREMIER LEAGUE WINS:	23
PREMIER LEAGUE GOALS SCORED:	74
QUICKEST GOAL SCORED:	11 SECONDS (VERSUS MANCHESTER UNITED)
QUICKEST GOAL CONCEDED:	3 MINUTES (VERSUS LIVERPOOL FC)
YELLOW/RED CARDS:	50/2
FIRST TEAM PLAYERS USED:	25

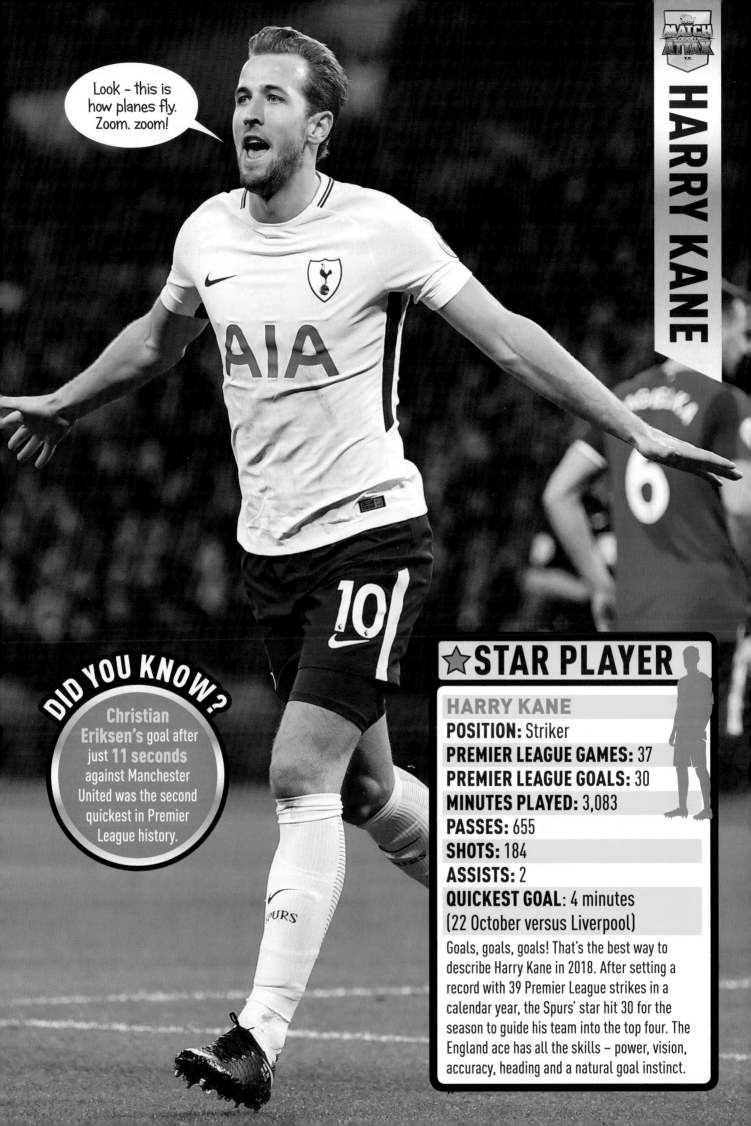

Look - this is how planes fly. Zoom, zoom!

HARRY KANE

DID YOU KNOW?

Christian Eriksen's goal after just **11 seconds** against Manchester United was the second quickest in Premier League history.

⭐ STAR PLAYER

HARRY KANE

POSITION: Striker
PREMIER LEAGUE GAMES: 37
PREMIER LEAGUE GOALS: 30
MINUTES PLAYED: 3,083
PASSES: 655
SHOTS: 184
ASSISTS: 2
QUICKEST GOAL: 4 minutes (22 October versus Liverpool)

Goals, goals, goals! That's the best way to describe Harry Kane in 2018. After setting a record with 39 Premier League strikes in a calendar year, the Spurs' star hit 30 for the season to guide his team into the top four. The England ace has all the skills – power, vision, accuracy, heading and a natural goal instinct.

LIVERPOOL FC

Jurgen Klopp's entertaining team enjoyed loads of exciting games in 2018. Take a closer look at The Reds and their superstar players!

TACTICS TALK

With an epic attacking trio of Mohamed Salah, Roberto Firmino and Sadio Mane, The Reds rocked the Premier League and were the second highest goal scorers in 2017-18. Manager Klopp usually started with a 4-3-3 set up, with Virgil Van Dijk controlling the defence and captain Jordan Henderson bossing central midfield. Alex Oxlade-Chamberlain enjoyed more game time after Philippe Coutinho joined Barcelona.

3 SICK STARS

ROBERTO FIRMINO The slick-skilled Brazilian has become a top-class No.9 for The Reds with his pace and penalty box skills.

ALEX OXLADE-CHAMBERLAIN Liverpool paid £35 million for the versatile midfielder. He's worth every penny with his non-stop running and goal threat.

JORDAN HENDERSON He skippers the team very well, making vital tackles and precise passes to release Liverpool's lightning-quick attackers.

STAR TO WATCH IN 2019
TRENT ALEXANDER-ARNOLD

The young defender was born in Liverpool and is desperate to become a first-team regular for The Reds, the team he supported as a boy. Alexander-Arnold has mostly played as right-back, but he could star in central midfield in the future.

Sssh! I'm awesome, but let's keep it a secret.

PAST HERO
STEVEN GERRARD

UEFA Champions League, FA Cup, League Cup, UEFA Super Cup – former Liverpool FC captain Steven Gerrard has bags of silverware! Between 1998 and 2015, the central midfielder scored 120 league goals and 41 in Europe. Stevie G mixed power, vision and quality passing to awesome affect for The Reds.

SEASON STATS

POSITION: 4TH
PREMIER LEAGUE POINTS: 75
PREMIER LEAGUE WINS: 21
PREMIER LEAGUE GOALS SCORED: 84
QUICKEST GOAL SCORED: 3 MINUTES (VERSUS TOTTENHAM HOTSPUR)
QUICKEST GOAL CONCEDED: 3 MINUTES (VERSUS LEICESTER CITY)
YELLOW/RED CARDS: 44/1
FIRST TEAM PLAYERS USED: 27

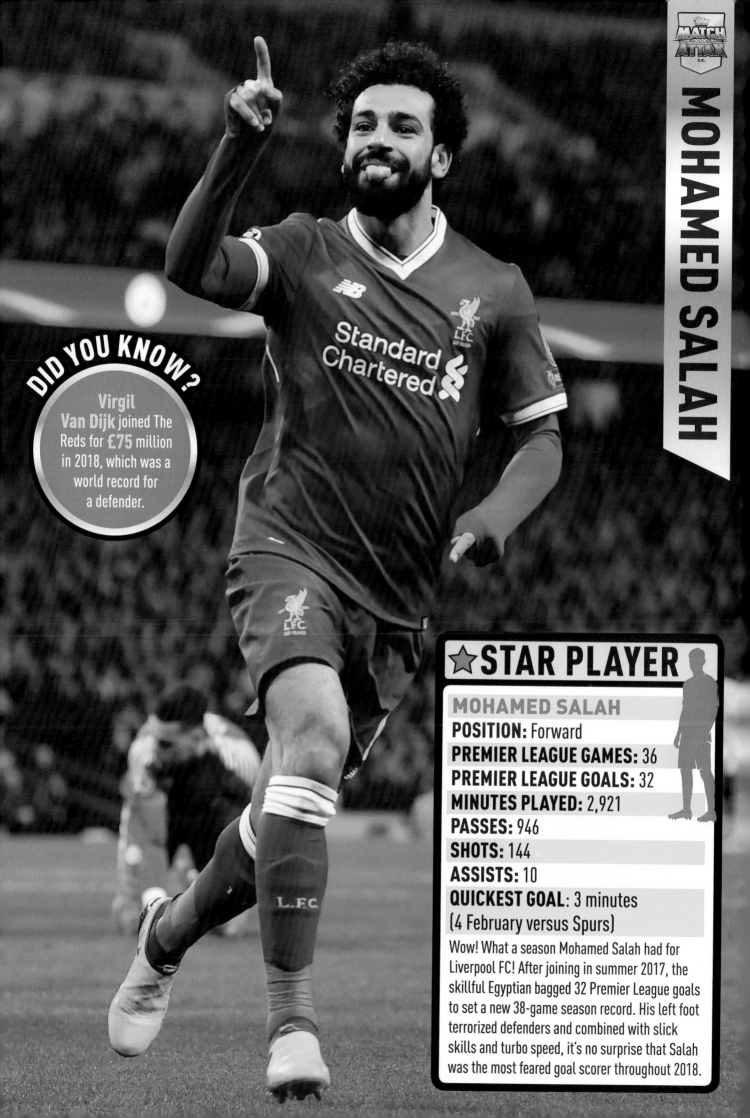

MOHAMED SALAH

DID YOU KNOW?

Virgil Van Dijk joined The Reds for £75 million in 2018, which was a world record for a defender.

☆ STAR PLAYER

MOHAMED SALAH

POSITION: Forward

PREMIER LEAGUE GAMES: 36

PREMIER LEAGUE GOALS: 32

MINUTES PLAYED: 2,921

PASSES: 946

SHOTS: 144

ASSISTS: 10

QUICKEST GOAL: 3 minutes (4 February versus Spurs)

Wow! What a season Mohamed Salah had for Liverpool FC! After joining in summer 2017, the skillful Egyptian bagged 32 Premier League goals to set a new 38-game season record. His left foot terrorized defenders and combined with slick skills and turbo speed, it's no surprise that Salah was the most feared goal scorer throughout 2018.

CHELSEA

The Blues are five-times Premier League champions and have a squad that's packed with world-class heroes.

TACTICS TALK

For the last couple of years, Chelsea have started with three centre-backs and used commanding defenders like Gary Cahill, Cesar Azpilicueta, Andreas Christensen and Antonio Rudiger to protect their goal. Marcos Alonso and Victor Moses operate as wing-backs, with N'Golo Kante the key holding midfielder. Willian, Pedro, Cesc Fabregas and Danny Drinkwater all compete for spots alongside Eden Hazard and Alvaro Morata.

STAR TO WATCH IN 2019

ROSS BARKLEY

Injury meant the England midfielder hardly played for Chelsea after joining from Everton in January. When he's fully fit, the £15 million man loves to boss the pitch and break forward to support attacks. Big things are expected of this exciting player!

3 SICK STARS

THIBAUT COURTOIS He's still only in his mid 20s, but Courtois controls his goal with incredible saves and reflexes.

ALVARO MORATA The former Juventus and Real Madrid striker is a beast in the box and loves taking defenders on one-on-one.

WILLIAN The busy Brazilian is always full of energy, skill and pace. He strikes a sweet free-kick with his right boot, too!

PAST HERO FRANK LAMPARD

Goal scoring midfielder Lampard played for The Blues from 2001 to 2014. In that time he clocked up 648 games, bagged a record 211 goals and secured 11 major honours. Lamps is also the highest-scoring midfielder in Premier League history with 177 goals.

SEASON STATS

POSITION: 5TH
PREMIER LEAGUE POINTS: 70
PREMIER LEAGUE WINS: 21
PREMIER LEAGUE GOALS SCORED: 62
QUICKEST GOAL SCORED: 2 MINUTES (VERSUS STOKE CITY)
QUICKEST GOAL CONCEDED: 6 MINUTES (VERSUS WEST HAM UNITED)
YELLOW/RED CARDS: 42/4
FIRST TEAM PLAYERS USED: 26

EDEN HAZARD

DID YOU KNOW?

Olivier Giroud is an awesome header of the ball – 27 of his first 73 league goals were scored with his head.

I just swallowed a fly. Yum!

⭐ STAR PLAYER

EDEN HAZARD

POSITION: Midfielder
PREMIER LEAGUE GAMES: 34
PREMIER LEAGUE GOALS: 12
MINUTES PLAYED: 2,432
PASSES: 1,369
SHOTS: 71
ASSISTS: 4
QUICKEST GOAL: 3 minutes (20 Jan versus Brighton & Hove Albion)

Chelsea's terrific No.10 had another top season at Stamford Bridge! This talented playmaker is The Blues' creative force in midfield, starting attacks, slipping in the strikers and pinging precise passes into the box. The brilliant Belgian is also a cool penalty-taker and scored a cheeky 'Panenka' from the spot against Newcastle last season.

ARSENAL

Check out The Gunners' greatest players, plus all the stats, facts and stories you need to know from 2018!

TACTICS TALK

Arsenal mixed their formations up in 2017-18, using both three centre-backs and a flat back four at times. Hector Bellerin was a key outlet down the right, using his pace to break forward, and creative midfielders like Ramsey, Ozil and Mkhitaryan supported Aubameyang. Alexandre Lacazette and Danny Welbeck added firepower, even if they didn't always start games.

3 SICK STARS

MESUT OZIL A pass and assist master, the classy German midfielder signed a new Arsenal deal in 2018.

HECTOR BELLERIN He's one of the best right-backs in the Premier League with a string of top displays.

AARON RAMSEY A constant threat from midfield. Aaron Ramsey banged in his first hat-trick against Everton in February.

STAR TO WATCH IN 2019

REISS NELSON

The teenage forward enjoyed a breakthrough year in 2018, playing in the Premier League, Europa League and cups. The Londoner likes to use his speed and quick footwork to beat defenders and Arsenal's coaches think he's got a great future at The Emirates!

PAST HERO THIERRY HENRY

At The Emirates Stadium there's a statue of Thierry Henry – proof that the Frenchman's a true Arsenal legend! With a record 228 goals and countless incredible moments with the club, Henry is remembered as a slick and superhuman striker by the fans.

Thierry's the tops!

SEASON STATS

POSITION: 6TH
PREMIER LEAGUE POINTS: 63
PREMIER LEAGUE WINS: 19
PREMIER LEAGUE GOALS SCORED: 74
QUICKEST GOAL SCORED: 2 MINUTES (VERSUS LEICESTER CITY)
QUICKEST GOAL CONCEDED: 3 MINUTES (VERSUS SOUTHAMPTON)
YELLOW/RED CARDS: 57/2
FIRST TEAM PLAYERS USED: 30

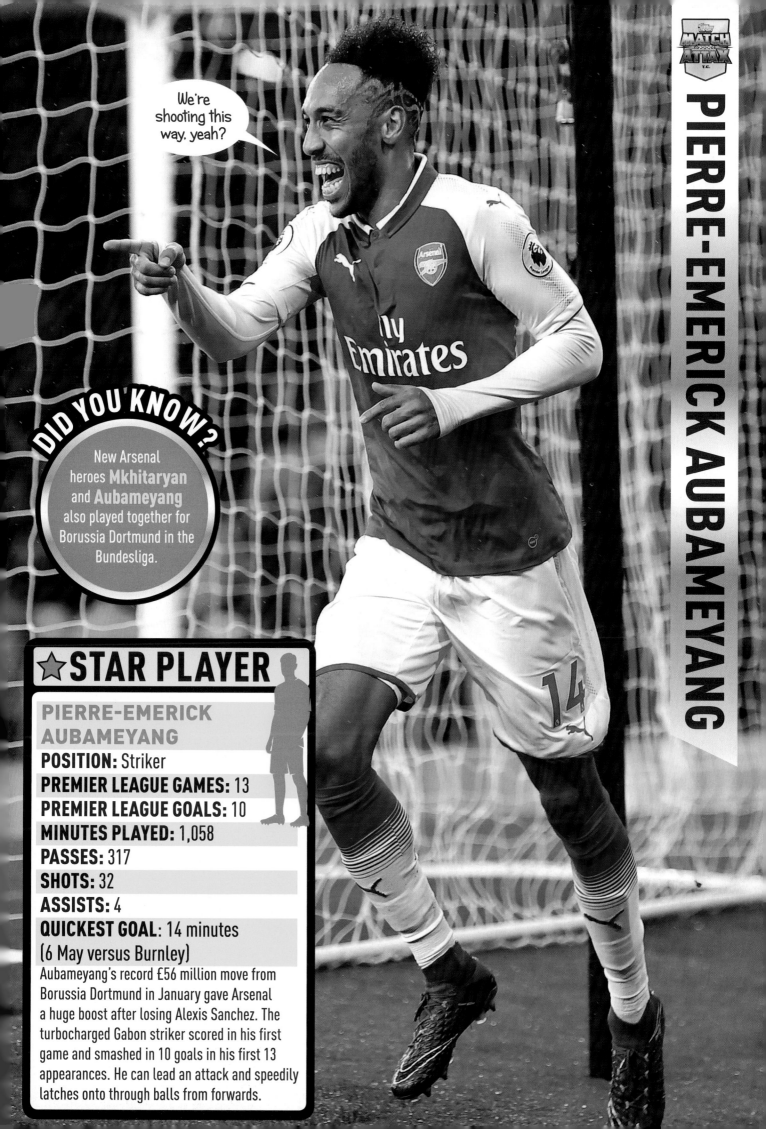

We're shooting this way, yeah?

PIERRE-EMERICK AUBAMEYANG

DID YOU KNOW?

New Arsenal heroes **Mkhitaryan** and **Aubameyang** also played together for Borussia Dortmund in the Bundesliga.

⭐ STAR PLAYER

PIERRE-EMERICK AUBAMEYANG

POSITION: Striker

PREMIER LEAGUE GAMES: 13

PREMIER LEAGUE GOALS: 10

MINUTES PLAYED: 1,058

PASSES: 317

SHOTS: 32

ASSISTS: 4

QUICKEST GOAL: 14 minutes (6 May versus Burnley)

Aubameyang's record £56 million move from Borussia Dortmund in January gave Arsenal a huge boost after losing Alexis Sanchez. The turbocharged Gabon striker scored in his first game and smashed in 10 goals in his first 13 appearances. He can lead an attack and speedily latches onto through balls from forwards.

BURNLEY

Burnley's fourth Premier League season was the club's best, finishing seventh and winning praise as well as lots of points!

TACTICS TALK

Burnley boss Sean Dyche made great use of his preferred 4-4-2 formation. His front pairing of Chris Wood and Ashley Barnes proved a big threat, and the pair bagged 19 goals between them by the end of the season. Jack Cork caught the eye in central midfield and Aaron Lennon was a livewire on the wing since moving from Everton. Centre-back James Tarkowski's awesome form won him his first England cap!

3 SICK STARS

NICK POPE The keeper came in for the injured Tom Heaton in 2017 and was fantastic. His super saves even earned him an England call-up.

JOHANN BERG GUDMUNDSSON The Iceland winger has stacks of cool skills and played over 30 Premier League games as Burnley finished seventh.

JEFF HENDRICK His passing, control and vision keep Burnley ticking in midfield. He plays close to the strikers and connects with headers and loose balls.

STAR TO WATCH IN 2019
STEVEN DEFOUR

The Belgium midfielder picked up a knee injury in January 2018, but he's desperate to get back in the Burnley team and mix it with the Premier League's best again. Defour's a class act and always drives The Clarets forward.

PAST HERO GLENN LITTLE

The thrilling right winger ripped it up for Burnley between 1997 and 2004, making over 280 club appearances. Little helped The Clarets win promotion to the old First Division and lit up Turf Moor with his electric runs and crossing.

SEASON STATS

POSITION: 7TH
PREMIER LEAGUE POINTS: 54
PREMIER LEAGUE WINS: 14
PREMIER LEAGUE GOALS SCORED: 36
QUICKEST GOAL SCORED: 3 MINUTES (VERSUS CRYSTAL PALACE & MANCHESTER UNITED)
QUICKEST GOAL CONCEDED: 6 MINUTES (VERSUS LEICESTER CITY)
YELLOW/RED CARDS: 65/0
FIRST TEAM PLAYERS USED: 24

CHRIS WOOD

Wood you believe these skills!

⭐STAR PLAYER

CHRIS WOOD

POSITION: Striker
PREMIER LEAGUE GAMES: 24
PREMIER LEAGUE GOALS: 10
MINUTES PLAYED: 1,633
PASSES: 415
SHOTS: 39
ASSISTS: 1
QUICKEST GOAL: 3 minutes (10 September versus Crystal Palace)

With a £15 million price tag, New Zealand striker Chris Wood has been worth every penny! With his powerful style and shooting, he scored important goals against Spurs, West Ham United and AFC Bournemouth, plus vital winners against Crystal Palace, Everton and West Bromwich Albion. Inside the box or holding up the ball, Wood is always a real handful!

DID YOU KNOW?

Burnley striker **Sam Vokes** scored for Wales in their EURO 2016 quarter-final win against Belgium.

EVERTON

The Toffees will be disappointed with their eighth place finish in 2018 as their talented team looks to rise high in the Premier League!

TACTICS TALK

Everton had lots of options in midfield in 2017-18. Idrissa Gueye was a defensive rock, snapping and tackling at the opposition, with Morgan Schneiderlin and Tom Davies also playing over 30 games. Going forward, Theo Walcott, Gylfi Sigurdsson, Yannick Bolasie and Wayne Rooney supported Cenk Tosun, Oumar Niasse or Dominic Calvert-Lewin.

3 SICK STARS

THEO WALCOTT From the right wing or just behind the striker, the ex-Arsenal ace created havoc with his speed and dazzling dribbling.

PHIL JAGIELKA Even in his mid-30s, 'Jags' is still Everton's best defender and will block, tackle and head anything in his path!

JORDAN PICKFORD The England keeper enjoyed a fine first season with Everton, pulling off top saves and keeping 10 clean sheets in the league.

STAR TO WATCH IN 2019
DOMINIC CALVERT-LEWIN

The powerful young goal scorer has competition for places in attack, but he's got the skills to become a first-team star. 'DCL' can play across the front, but also has the height to be a great target man.

PAST HERO
NEVILLE SOUTHALL

The finest goalkeeper ever to play for Everton, the big Welshman made a record 750 club appearances in the 1980s and '90s. Southall's flying saves and lightning reflexes helped The Toffees to two league titles, two FA Cups and the European Cup Winners' Cup.

SEASON STATS

POSITION: 8TH
PREMIER LEAGUE POINTS: 49
PREMIER LEAGUE WINS: 13
PREMIER LEAGUE GOALS SCORED: 44
QUICKEST GOAL SCORED: 6 MINUTES (VERSUS CRYSTAL PALACE)
QUICKEST GOAL CONCEDED: 1 MINUTE (VERSUS CRYSTAL PALACE)
YELLOW/RED CARDS: 51/3
FIRST TEAM PLAYERS USED: 30

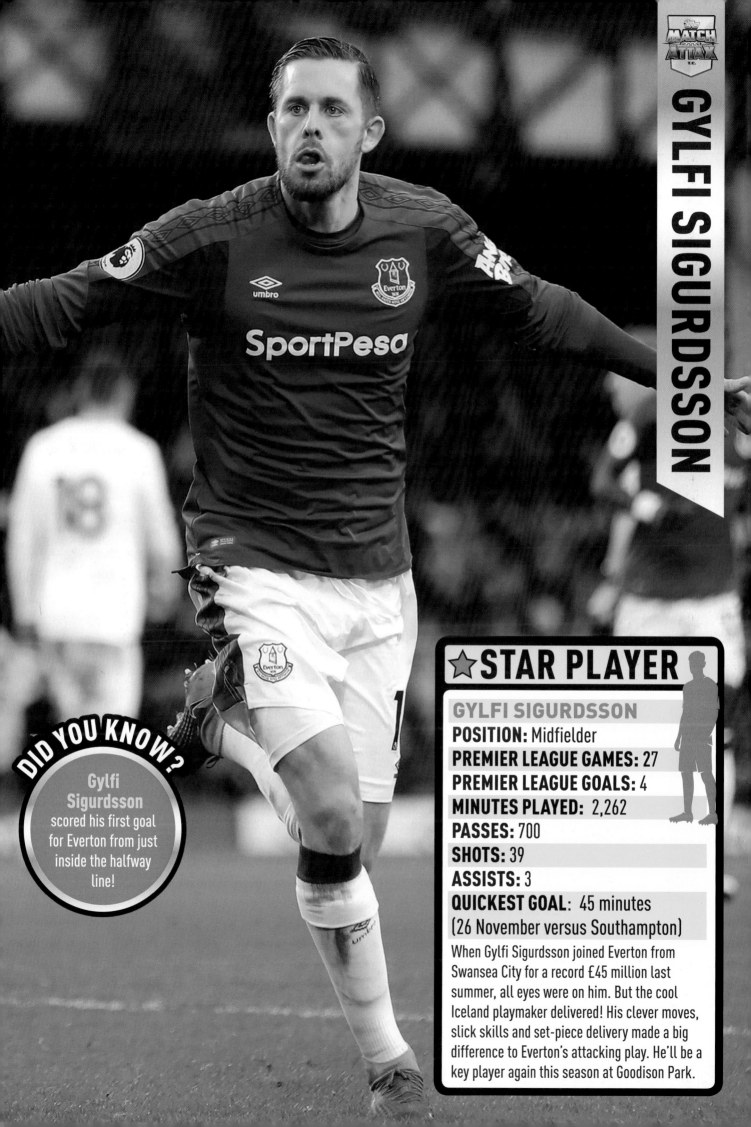

GYLFI SIGURDSSON

MATCH ATTAX

☆ STAR PLAYER

GYLFI SIGURDSSON

POSITION: Midfielder
PREMIER LEAGUE GAMES: 27
PREMIER LEAGUE GOALS: 4
MINUTES PLAYED: 2,262
PASSES: 700
SHOTS: 39
ASSISTS: 3
QUICKEST GOAL: 45 minutes
(26 November versus Southampton)

When Gylfi Sigurdsson joined Everton from Swansea City for a record £45 million last summer, all eyes were on him. But the cool Iceland playmaker delivered! His clever moves, slick skills and set-piece delivery made a big difference to Everton's attacking play. He'll be a key player again this season at Goodison Park.

DID YOU KNOW?

Gylfi Sigurdsson scored his first goal for Everton from just inside the halfway line!

LEICESTER CITY

Premier League champions in 2016, Leicester City fought hard for a top ten finish in 2018. Find out all The Foxes' top facts and stats.

TACTICS TALK

In 2017-18, manager Claude Puel still used a counter-attacking style that saw The Foxes shoot to the title two years earlier. However, his team are also happy to build play up slowly, before unleashing Jamie Vardy to burst into the box. Wes Morgan and Harry Maguire are a fortress in defence and Portuguese playmaker Adrien Silva distributes the ball very wisely.

3 SICK STARS

HARRY MAGUIRE A tough tackler, Maguire can also ping an accurate pass right from the back. His £17 million fee looks a bargain now!

WILFRED NDIDI Easily Leicester City's most impressive central midfielder. The Nigerian is mega powerful and always pressures the opposition.

KASPER SCHMEICHEL With over 40 clean sheets in the Premier League, The Foxes' No.1 loves to clear the danger with a flying save or punch!

STAR TO WATCH IN 2019

DEMARAI GRAY

The young winger has been at the King Power Stadium since 2016, but this could finally be his time to shine. The ex-Birmingham star can play on either wing or behind the striker and if he nails a position for Leicester City, Gray could really fly into form!

PAST HERO

CLAUDIO RANIERI

The likeable Italian managed Leicester City to a shock championship crown. The former Chelsea, Juventus and Inter Milan boss won praise for his quick counter-attacks and for making superstars of players like Jamie Vardy, Riyad Mahrez and N'Golo Kante.

SEASON STATS

POSITION: 9TH
PREMIER LEAGUE POINTS: 47
PREMIER LEAGUE WINS: 12
PREMIER LEAGUE GOALS SCORED: 56
QUICKEST GOAL SCORED: 1 MINUTE (VERSUS BRIGHTON & HOVE ALBION)
QUICKEST GOAL CONCEDED: 2 MINUTES (VERSUS ARSENAL)
YELLOW/RED CARDS: 52/5
FIRST TEAM PLAYERS USED: 27

JAMIE VARDY

⭐STAR PLAYER

JAMIE VARDY

POSITION: Striker
PREMIER LEAGUE GAMES: 37
PREMIER LEAGUE GOALS: 20
MINUTES PLAYED: 3,255
PASSES: 462
SHOTS: 70
ASSISTS: 1
QUICKEST GOAL: 3 minutes (20 December versus Liverpool FC)

In 2018, Vardy once again highlighted his natural skill and deadly goal scoring instinct. In 37 games for Leicester he cracked in 20 goals to take his overall Premier League record to 62 in 142 appearances. The England marksman uses speed, strength and a never-ending engine to beat the opposition and power the ball home.

NEWCASTLE UNITED

After promotion from the Championship, The Magpies rose to a comfortable mid-table finish in 2018. Check out the players who did the business in the Premier League!

TACTICS TALK

Boss Rafa Benitez changed his tactics and formations depending on the opposition. Against the top sides, The Magpies packed the midfield and defence, but deserve praise for attacking those teams closer to them in the table. Although Newcastle United only scored 39 goals, Dwight Gayle, Joselu and Ayoze Perez worked hard in attack and Jonjo Shelvey used his laser-guided passing to release the forwards.

3 SICK STARS

DEANDRE YEDLIN Newcastle United's first-choice right-back, the USA international can defend and attack with speed and style.

MATT RITCHIE The Scotland star can unleash great wing play. Ritchie reached five assists for the season and scored three goals.

JONJO SHELVEY The former Liverpool ace has a deadly mix of passing and tackling skills. When Shelvey's in top gear, The Magpies are a top team.

PAST HERO ALAN SHEARER

Every Newcastle United and Premier League fan knows what an epic goal scorer Shearer was. After joining The Magpies in 1996, 'Big Al' went on to hit 148 Premier League strikes, with 260 in total, and is the club's all-time top scorer with 206 goals in all competitions.

STAR TO WATCH IN 2019

JACOB MURPHY

Signed from Norwich City for £12 million, hopefully eye-catching winger Jacob Murphy's second season at St. James Park will see him show off his attacking skills. Murphy's magical boots have much more to offer.

I'm magic Murphy!

SEASON STATS

POSITION: 10TH
PREMIER LEAGUE POINTS: 44
PREMIER LEAGUE WINS: 12
PREMIER LEAGUE GOALS SCORED: 39
QUICKEST GOAL SCORED: 2 MINUTES
(VERSUS SOUTHAMPTON)
QUICKEST GOAL CONCEDED: 2 MINUTES
(VERSUS WATFORD)
YELLOW/RED CARDS: 52/2
FIRST TEAM PLAYERS USED: 27

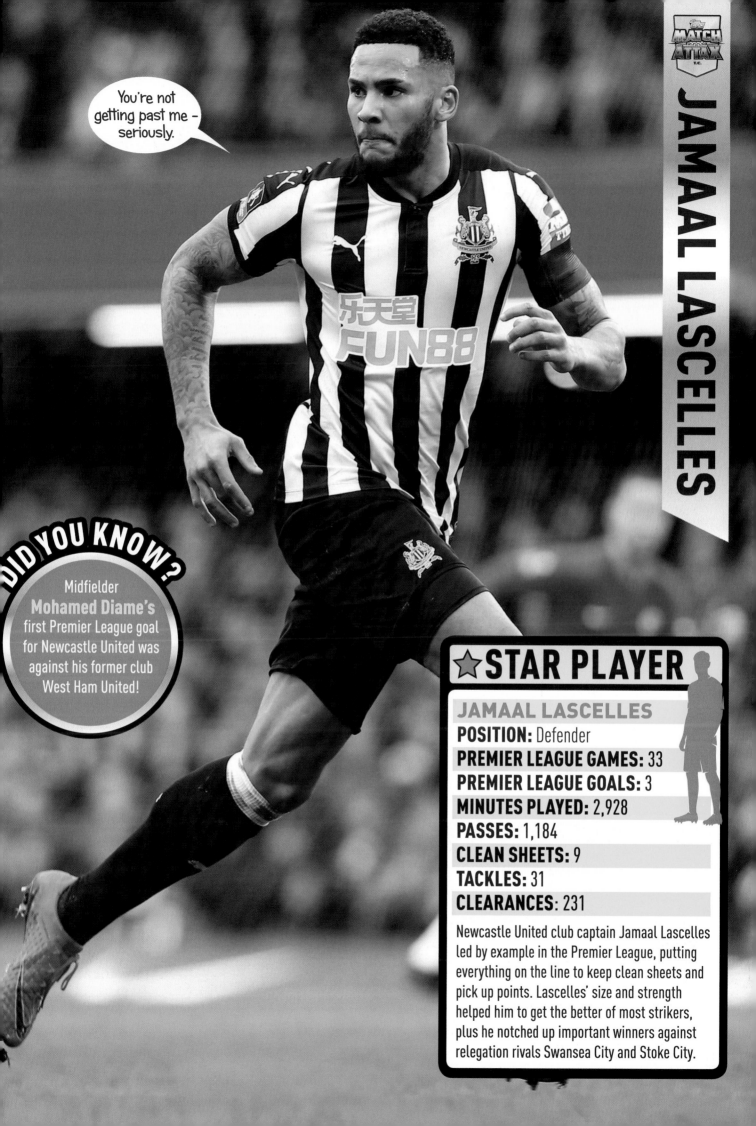

You're not getting past me – seriously.

JAMAAL LASCELLES

DID YOU KNOW?

Midfielder **Mohamed Diame's** first Premier League goal for Newcastle United was against his former club West Ham United!

⭐ STAR PLAYER

JAMAAL LASCELLES

POSITION: Defender
PREMIER LEAGUE GAMES: 33
PREMIER LEAGUE GOALS: 3
MINUTES PLAYED: 2,928
PASSES: 1,184
CLEAN SHEETS: 9
TACKLES: 31
CLEARANCES: 231

Newcastle United club captain Jamaal Lascelles led by example in the Premier League, putting everything on the line to keep clean sheets and pick up points. Lascelles' size and strength helped him to get the better of most strikers, plus he notched up important winners against relegation rivals Swansea City and Stoke City.

CRYSTAL PALACE

After starting the season with seven defeats, Roy Hodgson soon turned Crystal Palace around and took The Eagles to Premier League safety. Check out their stats and stars.

TACTICS TALK

To keep Crystal Palace on the attack, Hodgson got the best out of players like Andros Townsend, Ruben Loftus-Cheek and Luka Milivojevic. Mamadou Sakho and James Tomkins were awesome in central defence and Yohan Cabaye kept a cool head in central midfield. Striker Christian Benteke scored just three league goals, but worked like a battering ram up front, winning 236 aerial battles.

3 SICK STARS

LUKA MILIVOJEVIC The captain used his wits and cool set-piece skills to keep The Eagles in the Premier League. He scored seven crucial penalties.

JAMES TOMKINS With a cool 213 clearances, 47 tackles and eight clean sheets, there's no doubt that Tomkins was the standout defender.

ANDROS TOWNSEND The Eagles' top assist-maker created seven league goals. His dribbling, passing and crossing were hugely important at Selhurst Park.

PAST HERO IAN WRIGHT

Don't just think that goal machine Ian Wright is an Arsenal legend – he's a Crystal Palace hero too! In the 1980s and '90s, he scored 117 goals for The Eagles, winning promotion and a FA Cup runners' up medal. Fast, tricky and always ready to shoot, Wright was a right handful.

STAR TO WATCH IN 2019

ALEXANDER SORLOTH

In his first full season with Crystal Palace, the giant Norway striker will show his talent in front of goal. He has the power to put defenders on the floor and blast rocket shots into the net. Watch out for Sorloth in action!

SEASON STATS

POSITION: 11TH
PREMIER LEAGUE POINTS: 44
PREMIER LEAGUE WINS: 11
PREMIER LEAGUE GOALS SCORED: 45
QUICKEST GOAL SCORED: 1 MINUTE (VERSUS EVERTON)
QUICKEST GOAL CONCEDED: 3 MINUTES (VERSUS BURNLEY, MANCHESTER UNITED, NEWCASTLE UNITED)
YELLOW/RED CARDS: 72/0
FIRST TEAM PLAYERS USED: 28

WILFRIED ZAHA

I'm sorry, but this ball is all mine.

☆ STAR PLAYER

WILFRIED ZAHA

POSITION: Midfielder
PREMIER LEAGUE GAMES: 29
PREMIER LEAGUE GOALS: 9
MINUTES PLAYED: 2,551
PASSES: 623
SHOTS: 64
ASSISTS: 3
QUICKEST GOAL: 5 minutes (14 April versus Brighton & Hove Albion)

Zaha was the creative spark as The Eagles flew away from the drop zone. A quick and skillful attacker, he scored nine Premier League goals and made three assists and 76 crosses. Zaha's winner over Chelsea and goals against Brighton & Hove Albion, AFC Bournemouth and West Ham United gave the south Londoners a huge boost.

DID YOU KNOW?

Crystal Palace lost their first seven league games, and didn't score a goal, but still finished 11th!

AFC BOURNEMOUTH

Eddie Howe's Bournemouth easily saw off any relegation worries in 2018. Let's look at the reasons why The Cherries continue their Premier League journey!

TACTICS TALK

The Cherries enjoyed seeing young stars Ibe and Lewis Cook hold down first-team slots in 2018. Cook's energetic style in central midfield allowed Jordan Ibe and others like Junior Stanislas, Andrew Surman and Ryan Fraser to press forward. Jermain Defoe bagged a few key goals and Nathan Ake, a £20 million buy from Chelsea, beefed up AFC Bournemouth's defence.

3 SICK STARS

ASMIR BEGOVIC The keeper kept six clean sheets and played every Premier League game as AFC Bournemouth lost just once between Boxing Day and early March.

NATHAN AKE He made many well-timed tackles and used his aerial power to keep danger away from The Cherries' goal.

JOSH KING Not only did he have a direct hand in 11 Premier League goals, but he also coolly tucked away two very useful penalties.

STAR TO WATCH IN 2019

LEWIS COOK

With 2018 being Cook's breakthrough Premier League year, 2019 could be the year he becomes one of Europe's hottest young midfielders! If Cook can grab a few goals to go with his tactical awareness and passing, he'll be the complete package.

PAST HERO

JERMAIN DEFOE

That's right – deadly striker Defoe is both a past and current hero! When he was a teenager, Defoe scored 18 league goals on loan at AFC Bournemouth from West Ham United. He returned to the club in the summer of 2017 – he loves it on the south coast!

SEASON STATS

POSITION: 12TH
PREMIER LEAGUE POINTS: 44
PREMIER LEAGUE WINS: 11
PREMIER LEAGUE GOALS SCORED: 45
QUICKEST GOAL SCORED: 10 MINUTES (VERSUS CRYSTAL PALACE)
QUICKEST GOAL CONCEDED: 5 MINUTES (VERSUS BRIGHTON & HOVE ALBION, STOKE CITY)
YELLOW/RED CARDS: 55/1
FIRST TEAM PLAYERS USED: 22

JORDAN IBE

DID YOU KNOW?

At **163cm**, flying winger **Ryan Fraser** was the smallest player in the Premier League in 2017-18.

I'm the pick of The Cherries.

☆STAR PLAYER

JORDAN IBE

POSITION: Midfielder
PREMIER LEAGUE GAMES: 32
PREMIER LEAGUE GOALS: 2
MINUTES PLAYED: 2,000
PASSES: 693
SHOTS: 54
ASSISTS: 6
QUICKEST GOAL: 74 minutes (14 January versus Arsenal)

Jordan Ibe's second season on the south coast, following his £15 million switch from Liverpool FC, saw the tricky young winger really hit the highs. In 2017-18 he was The Cherries' assist king with six in the Premier League. Ibe also struck his first league goals, with a winner against Arsenal and a long-distance beauty in a 2-1 win over West Bromwich Albion.

GREATEST GOALS OF THE SEASON!

Er. who turned the lights off?

Volleys, long-range strikes, speedy counter attacks, solo dribbles... all sorts of spectacular goals were scored in the Premier League! Take a look at some of the best of the best.

JESSE LINGARD

WATFORD V MANCHESTER UNITED

The England midfielder has scored few special strikes for his club, but this is hard to beat. Lingard began running with the ball in his own half, blitzed past three players and fired low to the right of the keeper. Pure quality!

WAYNE ROONEY

EVERTON V WEST HAM UNITED

What a special goal this was! The Everton hero floated a long-range beauty from the centre circle, over the heads of two West Ham United defenders and goalkeeper Joe Hart. It was also Wayne's first hat-trick for the club in a brilliant 4-0 win.

KEVIN DE BRUYNE
LEICESTER CITY V MANCHESTER CITY

De Bruyne's rocket shot came at the end of a quick counter-attack. Leicester City had just struck City's post, but it was cleared to Kev, who played a speedy pass out to Leroy Sane. De Bruyne raced forward and controlled a pass on the edge of the area and fired a left foot belter into the top corner!

Obiang bangs it in!

CHARLIE DANIELS
AFC BOURNEMOUTH V MANCHESTER CITY

On a hot August afternoon, The Cherries' star struck an absolute scorcher against Manchester City! Daniels smacked a lethal, rising left foot shot from an angle on the edge of the box that zipped past Ederson.

PEDRO OBIANG
SPURS V WEST HAM UNITED

The Hammers' midfielder hardly ever scores, but this strike was unforgettable! He took two touches outside the box and smashed a stunning long-ranger past Hugo Lloris. Perfect placement from Pedro!

JAMIE VARDY

LEICESTER CITY V SPURS

Vardy set Leicester City on their way to a great 2-1 win with an acrobatic volley in the box. Albrighton looped the ball and Vardy leapt like a gymnast to poke it over Hugo Lloris. Another magical finish from The Foxes' goal king.

VICTOR WANYAMA

LIVERPOOL V SPURS

This power-packed shot nearly ripped the net in two! Spurs' menacing midfielder raced forward to snap a first-time rocket past keeper Karius in a truly thrilling Premier League game.

Thank you Vardy much!

JERMAIN DEFOE

CRYSTAL PALACE V BOURNEMOUTH

Jermain Defoe's racked up over 160 Premier League goals, but this effort from the edge of the penalty box is one of his very best. He let the ball bounce, before lifting a laser-accurate half volley past a stunned Crystal Palace defence.

MOHAMED SALAH
LIVERPOOL FC V SPURS
In the 90th minute, superhuman Salah somehow wriggled into the box, waved his left foot and lifted a precise chip past the Tottenham Hostpur keeper. Anfield went completely bonkers!

What's that sound? It's the sound of GOALS!

ANTONIO VALENCIA
MANCHESTER UNITED V EVERTON
Valencia's more used to stopping goals rather than scoring them! Against Everton at Old Trafford, he met a curling pass outside the box with a power-packed right-foot volley. It won the Premier League Goal of the Month.

SOFIANE BOUFAL
SOUTHAMPTON V WEST BROMWICH ALBION
Lionel Messi would've been well pleased if he'd scored this skillful goal! Boufal picked up the ball in his own half, turned, jinked and dribbled towards The Baggies' net and placed a smart left-foot drive past Ben Foster. The Saints fans were stunned by Boufal's brilliance.

WEST HAM UNITED

The Hammers battled hard to keep their Premier League place, with their star players and manager David Moyes producing some big results. Read on for the story of their season.

TACTICS TALK

In the 2017-18 season, West Ham United usually set up with three centre-backs, four across midfield and two attackers in support of Marko Arnautovic. Manuel Lanzini, Andre Ayew and Joao Mario performed well behind the striker and Pablo Zabaleta and Arthur Masuaku brought width. When fit, Andy Carroll was still a power-packed aerial threat up front!

3 SICK STARS

MANUEL LANZINI The creative Argentina No.10 was directly involved with 11 league goals. His passing and crossing were a big danger.

MICHAIL ANTONIO Although troubled by injury, the versatile attacking midfielder always worried defenders and hit three goals.

MARK NOBLE The Hammers' captain kept the team ticking and fought fearlessly in midfield. He also made his 300th Premier League appearance.

STAR TO WATCH IN 2019

DECLAN RICE

The young Republic of Ireland defender played an impressive total of 26 games in 2017-18. Making 573 passes, 29 tackles, and 70 clearances, plus keeping 10 clean sheets, the powerful star could become a fans' fave at the London Stadium!

PAST HERO PAOLO DI CANIO

With 118 Premier League appearances and 47 goals, striker Di Canio quickly became a West Ham United legend between 1999 and 2003. The Italian's best goal for The Hammers was an acrobatic scissor kick against Wimbledon in 2000 – fans will never forget it!

Deadly Di Canio delivers again!

SEASON STATS

POSITION: 13TH
PREMIER LEAGUE POINTS: 42
PREMIER LEAGUE WINS: 10
PREMIER LEAGUE GOALS SCORED: 48
QUICKEST GOAL SCORED: 6 MINUTES (VERSUS CHELSEA & NEWCASTLE UNITED)
QUICKEST GOAL CONCEDED: 8 MINUTES (VERSUS LEICESTER CITY)
YELLOW/RED CARDS: 73/2
FIRST TEAM PLAYERS USED: 27

We've totally got the best tattoos!

MARKO ARNAUTOVIC

⭐ STAR PLAYER

MARKO ARNAUTOVIC

POSITION: Striker
PREMIER LEAGUE GAMES: 31
PREMIER LEAGUE GOALS: 11
MINUTES PLAYED: 2,322
PASSES: 684
SHOTS: 71
ASSISTS: 6
QUICKEST GOAL: 6 minutes (Versus Chelsea and Newcastle United)

With a £24 million price tag, the awesome Austrian Arnautovic delivered on his big-money move from Stoke City with 11 goals and six assists in 2017-18. His strikes in wins over Chelsea, Huddersfield Town, Watford and Southampton were crucial and his attacking skills and vision were the platform for The Hammers' climb to safety.

DID YOU KNOW?

Andy Carroll struck his **24th** headed Premier League goal in a 2-1 win against West Bromwich Albion.

WATFORD

With wins over Arsenal and Chelsea, plus draws with Liverpool and Spurs, Watford had a Premier League season full of surprises.

TACTICS TALK

With the protection of Abdoulaye Doucoure and Etienne Capoue in deep midfield positions, boss Javi Gracia allowed Tom Cleverly and the attacking Brazilian Richarlison to help Troy Deeney break down defences. Tricky winger Gerard Deulofeu had an instant impact on loan from Barcelona as he scored on his debut against Chelsea. Sebastien Prodl was The Hornets' key centre-back once again.

3 SICK STARS

RICHARLISON Impressed with his pace and skills after joining in 2017. The forward bagged 5 goals and 4 assists.

TOM CLEVERLEY With a Premier League winners' medal from his Manchester United days, the box-to-box midfielder keeps a cool head for Watford.

WILL HUGHES Got a first-team run towards the end of the season and should have more games to show off his huge potential in the middle of the pitch.

PAST HERO

JOHN BARNES

In the early and mid 1980s, John Barnes bombing down the wing was one of the best sights in English footy! Barnes made 296 appearances for Watford, winning promotion to the top flight and reaching the 1984 FA Cup final. He joined Liverpool FC in 1987.

STAR TO WATCH IN 2019

NATHANIEL CHALOBAH

Sadly, the energetic ex-Chelsea star picked up an early injury last season that ruined his campaign. When he's fully fit, The Hornets' will expect the central midfielder to become a regular once again and control games with his power. Defenders need to watch out!

SEASON STATS

POSITION: 14TH

PREMIER LEAGUE POINTS: 41

PREMIER LEAGUE WINS: 11

PREMIER LEAGUE GOALS SCORED: 44

QUICKEST GOAL SCORED: 2 MINUTES (VERSUS NEWCASTLE UNITED)

QUICKEST GOAL CONCEDED: 1 MINUTE (VERSUS MANCHESTER CITY)

YELLOW/RED CARDS: 63/4

FIRST TEAM PLAYERS USED: 29

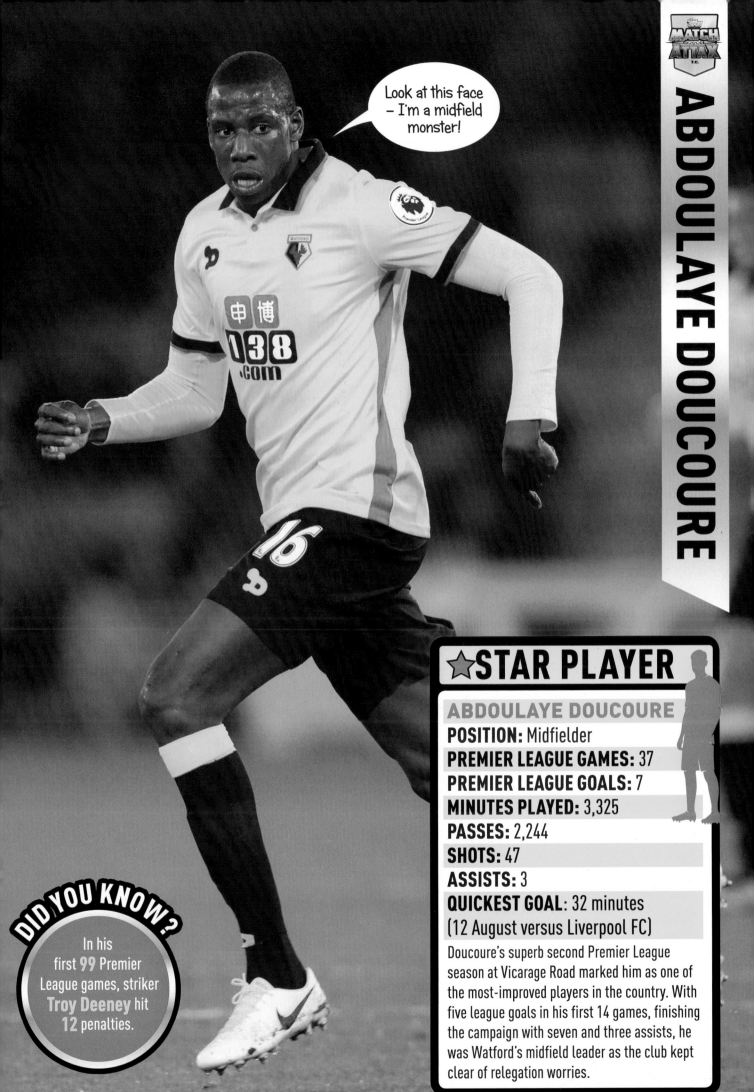

Look at this face – I'm a midfield monster!

ABDOULAYE DOUCOURE

DID YOU KNOW?

In his first **99** Premier League games, striker **Troy Deeney** hit **12** penalties.

⭐ STAR PLAYER

ABDOULAYE DOUCOURE

POSITION: Midfielder
PREMIER LEAGUE GAMES: 37
PREMIER LEAGUE GOALS: 7
MINUTES PLAYED: 3,325
PASSES: 2,244
SHOTS: 47
ASSISTS: 3
QUICKEST GOAL: 32 minutes
(12 August versus Liverpool FC)

Doucoure's superb second Premier League season at Vicarage Road marked him as one of the most-improved players in the country. With five league goals in his first 14 games, finishing the campaign with seven and three assists, he was Watford's midfield leader as the club kept clear of relegation worries.

BRIGHTON & HOVE ALBION

The Seagulls soared to a brilliant 15th place finish in 2018 in their first season in the Premier League. Find out who the south coast heroes are!

TACTICS TALK

Chris Hughton picked quite a settled team throughout 2017-18. He usually lined The Seagulls up in 4-4-1-1, with Murray supported by the gifted German Pascal Gross in attack. Wingers Jose Izquierdo and Anthony Knockaert whipped great crosses into the box and central midfielders Davy Propper and Dale Stephens played over 30 Premier League games. Hughton's defence was marshaled well by Lewis Dunk.

3 SICK STARS

PASCAL GROSS The former Bundesliga star was involved with 15 goals for Brighton & Hove Albion. His link-up with Murray worked wonders.

DAVY PROPPER The Dutch midfielder was class in his debut English season, creating three goals and winning 60 per cent of his tackles.

MAT RYAN He was always a super steady pair of hands protecting The Seagulls' net and played every league game.

STAR TO WATCH IN 2019

JURGEN LOCADIA

The deadly Dutch forward moved to Brighton & Hove Albion in January 2018 for a record fee that could reach £14 million. With a full season under his belt, Locadia wants to prove that he can be the top goal scorer at the AMEX Stadium.

Watch out for Big Bob!

SEASON STATS

POSITION: 15TH
PREMIER LEAGUE POINTS: 40
PREMIER LEAGUE WINS: 9
PREMIER LEAGUE GOALS SCORED: 34
QUICKEST GOAL SCORED: 5 MINUTES (VERSUS BOURNEMOUTH)
QUICKEST GOAL CONCEDED: 1 MINUTE (VERSUS LEICESTER CITY)
YELLOW/RED CARDS: 54/2
FIRST TEAM PLAYERS USED: 24

PAST HERO

BOBBY ZAMORA

In two spells on the south coast, the former West Ham United and Spurs striker smashed in 83 goals in 153 games. Zamora also won two England caps and hit 47 goals in 252 Premier League games. He would have loved to star for Brighton & Hove Albion in the top league!

I can stand on one leg longer than you!

GLENN MURRAY

DID YOU KNOW?

Unlucky defender **Lewis Dunk** scored **four** own goals in 2017-18, equaling the Premier League record.

⭐ **STAR PLAYER**

GLENN MURRAY

POSITION: Striker

PREMIER LEAGUE GAMES: 35

PREMIER LEAGUE GOALS: 12

MINUTES PLAYED: 2,196

PASSES: 664

SHOTS: 53

ASSISTS: 0

QUICKEST GOAL: 8 minutes (3 February versus West Ham United)

Before rejoining Brighton & Hove Albion in 2016, Murray was already a fans' fave at the club for scoring 56 goals in 136 games between 2008 to 2011. He lead The Seagulls' attack superbly in 2018, hitting the net 12 times, including scoring in big wins over West Ham United, Swansea City, Crystal Palace and Arsenal.

HUDDERSFIELD TOWN

With nine wins in their first Premier League season, The Terriers kept out of the bottom three to make sure they're battling the big boys again in 2019!

TACTICS TALK

David Wagner's team lost just three of their opening nine games last season with a mix of Championship heroes and top-quality new stars. Record signing Steve Mounie hit important goals and Belgium forward Laurent Depoitre bagged six to pick up points against Leicester, Manchester United, Watford and Southampton. Wagner's 4-2-3-1 kept them strong at the back and able to hit quick counter-attacks.

PAST HERO ANDY BOOTH

Booth is a true Huddersfield Town legend. Bagging 150 goals in two spells between 1992 to 1996 and 2001 to 2009, he won promotion to Division One and was lethal in the air and inside the box. Booth is now Club Ambassador and just as popular with the fans.

3 SICK STARS

STEVE MOUNIE The big Benin striker settled well in the Premier League. His opening day double against Crystal Palace set The Terriers up for the season!

JONATHAN HOGG He made over 100 tackles and won 70 per cent of them, adding bite to The Terriers' midfield.

CHRISTOPHER SCHINDLER Ice-cool at centre-back, the strong German can block, tackle and steal the ball from strikers. A key player for Huddersfield Town.

STAR TO WATCH IN 2019

TOM INCE

The skillful winger played over 30 league games last season, but in 2018-19 he wants to improve on his goal tally of just two strikes. Ince has amazing talent and will be threatening goalkeepers and forcing many more saves.

SEASON STATS

POSITION: 16TH
PREMIER LEAGUE POINTS: 37
PREMIER LEAGUE WINS: 9
PREMIER LEAGUE GOALS SCORED: 28
QUICKEST GOAL SCORED: 6 MINUTES (VERSUS WATFORD)
QUICKEST GOAL CONCEDED: 3 MINUTES (VERSUS ARSENAL)
YELLOW/RED CARDS: 62/3
FIRST TEAM PLAYERS USED: 25

AARON MOOY

DID YOU KNOW?
In their 0-0 with Swansea City, Huddersfield Town had **30** shots – the most by a Premier League team without scoring all season!

Can't. Stop. Sticking. Tongue. Out!

⭐ STAR PLAYER

AARON MOOY
POSITION: Midfielder
PREMIER LEAGUE GAMES: 36
PREMIER LEAGUE GOALS: 4
MINUTES PLAYED: 3,071
PASSES: 1,902
SHOTS: 29
ASSISTS: 3
QUICKEST GOAL: 23 minutes (16 December versus Watford)

With four goals and three assists, plus a string of standout displays, Australian Aaron Mooy made headlines all season for Huddersfield Town. The former Manchester City midfielder can pick the perfect pass and formed an exciting partnership with Jonathan Hogg. He opened the scoring in the memorable 2-1 win against Manchester United.

TOP SCOTS!

Celtic cruised to their seventh championship in a row, with Rangers and the rest battling hard behind them. Take a look at the Scottish facts and stats.

CELTIC

SEASON STATS

SCOTTISH TOP SCORER:
KRIS BOYD (KILMARNOCK) 18 GOALS

UEFA CHAMPIONS LEAGUE TOP SCORER:
GRIFFITHS/ROBERTS/SINCLAIR/McGREGOR/DEMBELE (CELTIC) 1 GOAL

SCOTTISH MANAGER OF THE SEASON:
BRENDAN RODGERS (CELTIC)

PLAYER OF THE SEASON:
SCOTT BROWN (CELTIC)

BEST YOUNG PLAYER:
KIERAN TIERNEY (CELTIC)

RELEGATED TEAMS:
PARTICK THISTLE
ROSS COUNTY

Celtic's unbeaten record in Scottish league and cup games ended in November, standing at 69 games, but they still won a treble of league, Scottish Cup and Scottish League Cup. Captain Scott Brown was the driving force again, with goal scorers Scott Sinclair, Leigh Griffiths, James Forrest and Moussa Dembele hitting double figures in all competitions. Versatile young defender Kieran Tierney captained Scotland for the very first time, too.

ABERDEEN

The Dons are one of the Premiership's top teams and began last season with just one league loss in their first 12 games. Young centre-back Scott McKenna was a star for Derek McInnes' side and won his first cap for Scotland. Striker Adam Rooney lead the line, bagging nine goals to take his club tally to 88 in 197 appearances.

RANGERS

The Gers couldn't keep hold of second place and finished third for the second season in a row. They lost four and drew one game against Glasgow rivals Celtic, but scored four or more goals in league wins over Dundee, Hamilton and St Johnstone. New Colombian striker Alfredo Morelos top scored with 14 goals and right-back James Tavernier had another impressive season at Ibrox.

HIBERNIAN

Entering the Premiership as Scottish Championship winners, manager Neil Lennon did a great job to keep Hibs around the league's top four places. Two draws with Celtic and a win at Rangers were the highlights. Winger Martin Boyle caught the eye at Easter Road, with playmaker Dylan McGeouch using his class and vision to control the midfield.

PREM PARTY!

After six seasons away from the Premier League, Wolverhampton Wanderers burst back into the big time in 2018!

1 MEGA MANAGER

Nuno Espirito Santo took Wolverhampton Wanderers into the Premier League in style! In his first job in English footy, the manager made the team the strongest in the league in attack and defence, losing just seven games all season. Watching Wolves tear into teams was a total joy!

2 AWESOME AFOBE

Striker Benik Afobe rejoined Wolves on loan from AFC Bournemouth in January, having blasted 23 in 48 games for the Molineux club. He struck six times, including goals in big wins over Leeds, Reading, Birmingham and Bolton, and the fans loved seeing him power the ball home. Afobe's move back to Wolves has made a big impact.

I forgot how to say cheese, so I'll just roar. RAAAR!

③ PORTUGAL POWER

The Portuguese manager picked up some star players from his home country. Forward Diogo Jota, midfielder Ruben Neves and defender Roderick Miranda joined goal scoring wingers Ivan Cavaleiro and Helder Costa at Molineux. Mixed with Brazilian striker Leo Bonatini, who speaks Portuguese, the imports helped shoot Wolves to the trophy.

④ GOALS, GOALS, GOALS

Wolves fired in 82 Championship goals in 2017-18, the most in the division. Jota, Bonatini, Costa, Neves and Cavaleiro cracked in 49 between them, with Romain Saiss and key defenders Matt Doherty and Barry Douglas also regularly hitting the net. Wing-back Douglas made an incredible 15 goal assists!

⑤ MAKING A POINT

Wolves were top of the Championship table since October, and were 12 points clear of second place with 15 games to go. They finished the season with 99 points, which didn't quite beat the 103 they collected by winning League 1 in 2014. By making big points in the Championship, they hope to stay well away from the Premier League drop zone!

DID YOU KNOW?
All **six** of **Ruben Neves'** goals last season were scored from outside the box.

CHAMPIONSHIP

Cardiff won a place in the Premier League after a terrific Championship season. Check out the league's best teams...

WELSH WONDERS!

SEASON STATS

CHAMPIONSHIP TOP SCORER:
MATEJ VYDRA (DERBY) 21 GOALS

MANAGER OF THE SEASON:
NUNO ESPIRITO SANTO

PLAYER OF THE SEASON:
RYAN SESSEGNON (FULHAM)

BEST YOUNG PLAYER:
RYAN SESSEGNON (FULHAM)

RELEGATED TEAMS:
BARNSLEY
BURTON ALBION
SUNDERLAND

CARDIFF CITY

Manager Neil Warnock inspired a fantastic season in the Welsh capital, leading Cardiff back to the Premier League after four seasons. They began with only one loss in 11 games, including a 2-1 win at Wolves. Defenders Sol Bamba and Sean Morrison were rocks at the back, allowing creative stars like Junior Hoilett and Kenneth Zahore to wreck havoc at the other end. Switching Callum Peterson from defence to midfield was a masterstroke by Warnock.

FULHAM

The London club won promotion the hard way! They saw off Derby in the play-off semi-finals and edged past Aston Villa 1-0 in the final at Wembley. The Cottagers have stars like teenage winger Ryan Sessegnon, striker Aleksandar Mitrovic and defender Denis Odoi to thank. Captain Tom Cairney scored the vital winner against Villa.

ASTON VILLA

Steve Bruce's team came close to reaching the Premier League after two seasons in the Championship. Their narrow loss to Fulham was tough. Albert Adomah was Villa's top scorer with 14 goals and creative stars Jack Grealish and Conor Hourihane bossed the centre. Young midfielder Keinan Davis will be one to watch in 2019.

MIDDLESBROUGH

Boro were narrowly beaten 1-0 by Aston Villa in the Championship play-off semi-finals, denying the north-east club an immediate return to the Premier League. Tony Pulis took charge at Christmas at The Riverside Stadium, winning 11 of his 22 league games to finish fifth with 76 points. Strikers Britt Assombalonga and Patrick Bamford hit 26 Championship goals between them.

It's time to showcase some of the Premier League's most talented youngsters – these teenagers could be the footy superstars of the future!

AWESOME ACADEMY STARS!

CALLUM HUDSON-ODOI, Chelsea
POSITION: Forward
BORN: November 7, 2000
Chelsea's youth teams have been very successful in recent years and Blues fans have high hopes for England youth star Hudson-Odoi. The speedy forward quickly progressed from the Under-18s to the Under-23s. His knack for hitting the net saw him make his Premier League debut against AFC Bournemouth.

Check my Spanish skills!

ARNAU PUIGMAL, Manchester United
POSITION: Midfielder
BORN: January 10, 2001
The silky-skilled Spanish youngster moved to Old Trafford in 2017 after the United coaches spotted his dazzling dribbling and passing moves. The teenager loves taking set pieces and scored a fantastic free-kick on his Under-18s debut against Newcastle in 2017-18.

OLIVER SKIPP, Tottenham Hotspur
POSITION: Midfielder
BORN: September 16, 2000
The classy central midfielder became a Spurs Under-18 regular when he was still a schoolboy! Born in Hertfordshire, Skipp's a combative player who breaks up attacks. He played every minute of the 2017-18 UEFA Youth League group stage, including a 3-2 win against Real Madrid!

TAYLOR RICHARDS, Manchester City
POSITION: Midfielder
BORN: December 3, 2000
With England Under-17 star Phil Foden already appearing in Pep Guardiola's first team, the next young Manchester City super kid could be Taylor Richards. He's a tricky winger or attacking central midfielder who scored three goals in his first four UEFA Youth League games in 2017.

KYLIAN MBAPPE
BORN: December 20, 1998
POSITION: Striker **PSG & FRANCE**
Fast, tricky and full of spectacular goals.

GIANLUIGI DONNARUMMA
BORN: February 25, 1999
POSITION: Keeper **AC MILAN & ITALY**
Giant shot-stopper with rocket reflexes.

I'm playing for my dream team!

MATTHIJS DE LIGT
BORN: August 12, 1999
POSITION: Centre-back **AJAX & HOLLAND**
Tough tackling and cool on the ball.

CURTIS JONES, Liverpool FC
POSITION: Midfielder
BORN: January 30, 2001
The box-to-box teenager first played for Liverpool FC at Under-9s level. The Under-18s academy team was built around Jones' clever midfield skills and the England Under-17 star scores a lot of goals, blasting 10 in his first 14 games in 2017-18. Jones even made the first-team squad last season.

JADON SANCHO
BORN: March 25, 2000
POSITION: Winger
BORUSSIA DORTMUND & ENGLAND U-19
Eye-catching forward with pace and creativity.

SOUTHAMPTON

Saints fans are hoping for better things in 2018-19, after just beating relegation on the final day! Take a look at their up-and-down campaign.

TACTICS TALK

Playing with a back three and wingbacks or a straight four in defence, Saints tried to outnumber the opposition and launch balls forward. But strikers Charlie Austin, Manolo Gabbiadini and Shane Long only grabbed 14 goals, leaving midfielders Dusan Tadic, James Ward-Prowse and Steven Davis to reach the box as much as possible. Alex McCarthy replaced Fraser Forster in goal and manager Mark Hughes hoped substitute Sofiane Boufal could repeat his wonderstrike against West Bromwich Albion.

3 SICK STARS

NATHAN REDMOND The lively winger worked tirelessly in defence and attack. Redmond had 44 shots in the season, more than any Saints player.

MARIO LEMINA On loan from Juventus, the combative midfielder gave strong performances, winning 55 tackles and 36 interceptions.

CHARLIE AUSTIN Scoring in wins over West Ham United and Everton, Austin finished the season as top scorer with seven goals. Strong on the ground and in the air.

STAR TO WATCH IN 2019

GUIDO CARRILLO

The Argentina ace could be the man to answer Southampton's scoring problems. He's had little opportunity since arriving for £19 million in January, but his goal power should see him scare off defenders every Saturday!

PAST HERO

MATTHEW LE TISSIER

Penalties, free-kicks, wonder strikes and clever tap-ins – magical Matt Le Tissier scored all sorts for Saints! With 100 Premier League goals and 64 assists, 'Le Tiss' wowed fans on the south coast until he retired in 2002. The forward remains one of the most creative and naturally talented players that the league has ever seen.

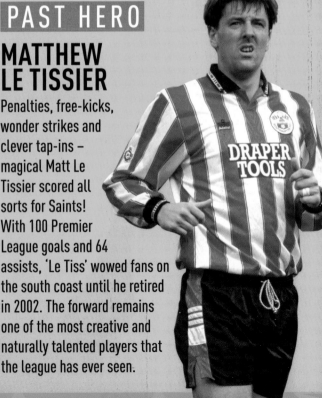

SEASON STATS

POSITION: 17TH
PREMIER LEAGUE POINTS: 36
PREMIER LEAGUE WINS: 7
PREMIER LEAGUE GOALS SCORED: 37
QUICKEST GOAL SCORED: 3 MINUTES (VERSUS ARSENAL)
QUICKEST GOAL CONCEDED: 2 MINUTES (VERSUS NEWCASTLE UNITED)
YELLOW/RED CARDS: 63/2
FIRST TEAM PLAYERS USED: 26

RYAN BERTRAND

⭐ STAR PLAYER

RYAN BERTRAND
POSITION: Defender
PREMIER LEAGUE GAMES: 35
PREMIER LEAGUE GOALS: 0
MINUTES PLAYED: 3,136
PASSES: 1,480
CLEAN SHEETS: 6
TACKLES: 48
CLEARANCES: 60

In a difficult season that saw Virgil Van Dijk leave for Liverpool FC, Ryan Bertrand became Southampton's most important defender. The energetic full-back sprinted up and down the left wing all season, making four assists, 136 crosses and boasting a 73 per cent tackle success. The England star helped Saints to keep six clean sheets.

SWANSEA CITY

The Swans couldn't keep their Premier League status and dropped out of the league on the final day of the season.

TACTICS TALK

Carlos Carvalhal took charge just after Christmas and soon wrapped up all three points with fantastic wins over Arsenal and Liverpool FC. He made Swansea City compact and defensive, playing with five, three and four at the back at times. Jordan Ayew popped up with some big goals, helped in attack by Tammy Abraham, Ki Sung-Yueng and Wilfried Bony.

3 SICK STARS

SAM CLUCAS Tidy midfielder with an eye for goal. All three of his strikes last season came against Arsenal!

TAMMY ABRAHAM On loan from Chelsea, the striker scored four in his first eight league games. Grabbed a great leveller against West Bromwich Albion.

KYLE NAUGHTON Worked tirelessly in defence and attacked down the right. He made the most tackles and interceptions for Swansea City last season.

STAR TO WATCH IN 2019

TOM CARROLL

The former Tottenham Hotspur man picked up his form at the end of 2017-18 and finished as the club's top goal creator with four assists. Carroll's determined to hit the highs again and be Swansea City's most magical midfielder in 2019.

PAST HERO LEON BRITTON

The intelligent former West Ham United man has played over 500 games for Swansea City. He's appeared in all four divisions for the club and picked up the League Cup in 2013. Britton was caretaker manager in December 2017.

SEASON STATS

POSITION: 18TH
PREMIER LEAGUE POINTS: 33
PREMIER LEAGUE WINS: 8
PREMIER LEAGUE GOALS SCORED: 28
QUICKEST GOAL SCORED: 3 MINUTES (VERSUS STOKE CITY)
QUICKEST GOAL CONCEDED: 4 MINUTES (VERSUS CHELSEA)
YELLOW/RED CARDS: 51/1
FIRST TEAM PLAYERS USED: 26

The Mawson-ator will rip it up!

DID YOU KNOW?

Andre Ayew is the older brother of Jordan Ayew. Forward Andre rejoined Swansea City in January 2018 from West Ham United for £18 million.

ALFIE MAWSON

⭐STAR PLAYER

ALFIE MAWSON

POSITION: Defender
PREMIER LEAGUE GAMES: 38
PREMIER LEAGUE GOALS: 2
MINUTES PLAYED: 3,420
PASSES: 1,744
TACKLES: 32
CLEAN SHEETS: 9
CLEARANCES: 222

With Swansea City needing to be mega tough at the back, Alfie Mawson was ultra reliable. He played every Premier League game and scored a shock winner against Liverpool FC. Mawson also helped keep clean sheets against relegation rivals Southampton, Crystal Palace, Huddersfield Town and West Bromwich Albion. He's a superb defensive leader.

STOKE CITY

The Potters enjoyed the Premier League party from 2008 to 2018. Here's a great guide to their final season in the top flight.

TACTICS TALK

Stoke City's tough defence and well organised teamwork used to be the foundation for their Premier League survival. Sadly, The Potters conceded 68 goals in 2017-18, the joint worst in the league, even though keeper Jack Butland worked mega hard. The team relied on the experience of players like Darren Fletcher, Charlie Adam, Ryan Shawcross and Erik Pieters to keep them safe.

3 SICK STARS

JACK BUTLAND An England regular, Butland pulled off some brilliant saves throughout Stoke City's 2017-18 season.

JOE ALLEN The Welshman has a fantastic passing range and great engine to get up and down the pitch.

ERIC MAXIM CHOUPO-MOTING A big hit in his first season at Stoke City. He scored twice in a 2-2 draw with Manchester United.

STAR TO WATCH IN 2019

TOM EDWARDS

Teenager Tom Edwards used to support Stoke City from the stands. In 2019, the England youth right-back could become a big fave with the fans if he's given a run in the first team. He has the tackling, crossing and energy levels to make the position his own!

PAST HERO RICARDO FULLER

Fans loved seeing Jamaican forward Ricardo Fuller dancing and dribbling with the ball! He arrived at Stoke City in 2006 and helped them win promotion to the Premier League for the first time. In total Fuller made 208 appearances and scored 50 goals.

Fuller's full of goals!

SEASON STATS

POSITION: 19TH
PREMIER LEAGUE POINTS: 33
PREMIER LEAGUE WINS: 7
PREMIER LEAGUE GOALS SCORED: 35
QUICKEST GOAL SCORED: 5 MINUTES (VERSUS AFC BOURNEMOUTH)
QUICKEST GOAL CONCEDED: 2 MINUTES (VERSUS CHELSEA)
YELLOW/RED CARDS: 62/1
FIRST TEAM PLAYERS USED: 30

DID YOU KNOW?

In November 2017, **Peter Crouch** scored a record **52nd** headed goal in the Premier League.

⭐ STAR PLAYER

XHERDAN SHAQIRI

POSITION: Midfielder

PREMIER LEAGUE GAMES: 36

PREMIER LEAGUE GOALS: 8

MINUTES PLAYED: 3,049

PASSES: 1,055

SHOTS: 69

ASSISTS: 7

QUICKEST GOAL: 5 minutes (3 February versus AFC Bournemouth)

Even though the Switzerland skill king was involved in 15 Premier League goals, he still couldn't save Stoke City from relegation. The exciting midfielder used his lethal left foot to blast past the keeper in three league games in a row in February 2018. He's only a little player, but he always makes a big impact on the pitch!

WEST BROMWICH ALBION

The Baggies enjoyed eight Premier League campaigns in a row from 2010 to 2018. Here's the story, facts and stats of their season.

TACTICS TALK

The Baggies' preferred 4-4-2 system used a powerful central midfield partnership of Jake Livermore and Chris Brunt, with the experience of Gareth Barry also playing a part. James McLean and Matt Phillips were the main threats out wide, with Salomon Rondon, Hal Robson-Kanu and Jay Rodriguez competing for the striking spots. Rondon's power was often used to force defences apart.

3 SICK STARS

JAY RODRIGUEZ The former Southampton striker never gives defenders a rest - he's a real livewire in the box.

AHMED HEGAZI The centre-back joined The Baggies permanently in 2017. Cool under constant pressure, his solid defensive skills stood out.

CHRIS BRUNT With a quality left foot, Brunt's delivery and passion in midfield has had a big influence on West Bromwich Albion's play.

STAR TO WATCH IN 2019
OLIVER BURKE

Signed for £15 million in 2017, the speedy winger struggled in the Premier League. But the Baggies hope that back in the Championship, where he played so well for his first club Nottingham Forest, his star quality will help them get back into the Premier League.

PAST HERO BRYAN ROBSON

Former England and Manchester United captain Robson began his glittering career at The Hawthorns. In the late 1970s he developed into one of the best young central midfielders in Europe, with box-to-box energy and a huge winning attitude.

SEASON STATS

POSITION: 20TH
PREMIER LEAGUE POINTS: 31
PREMIER LEAGUE WINS: 6
PREMIER LEAGUE GOALS SCORED: 31
QUICKEST GOAL SCORED: 4 MINUTES (VERSUS SPURS, BRIGHTON & HOVE ALBION, SOUTHAMPTON)
QUICKEST GOAL CONCEDED: 4 MINUTES (VERSUS LIVERPOOL)
YELLOW/RED CARDS: 73/1

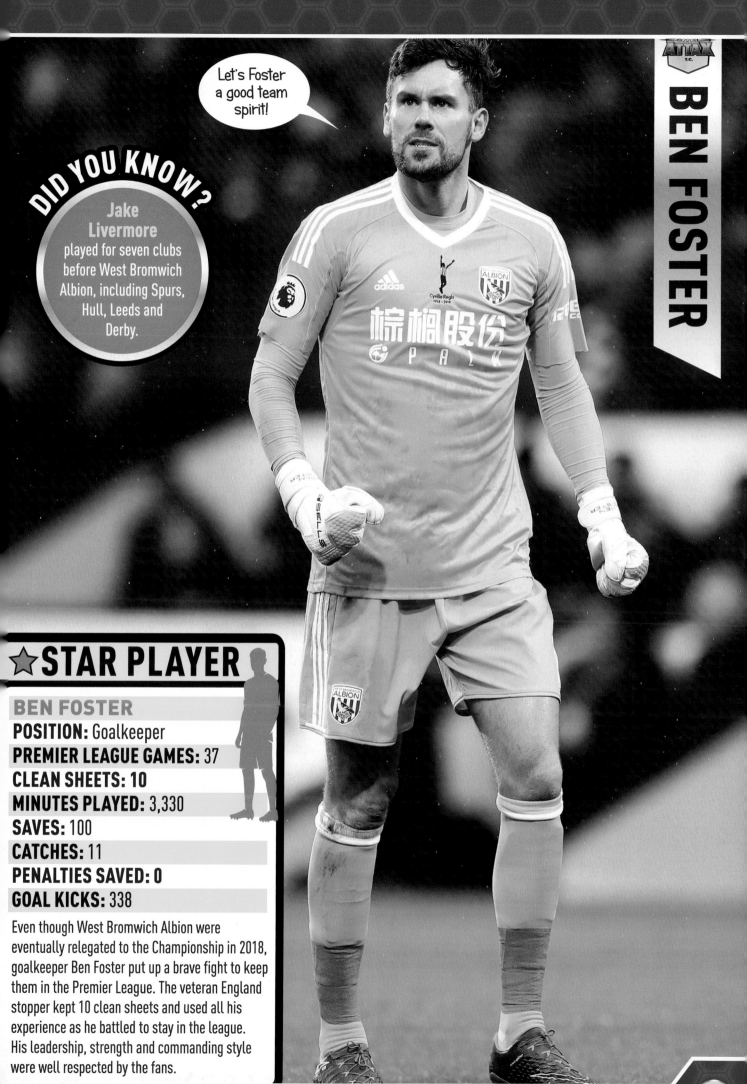

BEN FOSTER

Let's Foster a good team spirit!

DID YOU KNOW?

Jake Livermore played for seven clubs before West Bromwich Albion, including Spurs, Hull, Leeds and Derby.

⭐ STAR PLAYER

BEN FOSTER

POSITION: Goalkeeper
PREMIER LEAGUE GAMES: 37
CLEAN SHEETS: 10
MINUTES PLAYED: 3,330
SAVES: 100
CATCHES: 11
PENALTIES SAVED: 0
GOAL KICKS: 338

Even though West Bromwich Albion were eventually relegated to the Championship in 2018, goalkeeper Ben Foster put up a brave fight to keep them in the Premier League. The veteran England stopper kept 10 clean sheets and used all his experience as he battled to stay in the league. His leadership, strength and commanding style were well respected by the fans.

GOAL GREATS!

These goal aces all hit the net in 2018 – keep your eyes peeled to spot the lot!

```
E F Y A H H M V M S P K F S B A
F T Y E F J A A K F W S N A M O
R E T U N G Q I R A V A Z N L B
W M D E U O L A U T E W F C X B
N O S E Z Y O B Q V I T D H F G
L E R P A A A R R S F A J E T M
Z O A R I M C J O R H U L Z P C
T S R N E K O A V I R O S X R S
L U A Y N N N K L U K N Q M L C
M B A L I A T A R O M Z G V S B
V N Y M A I M Z M Z B U N T U O
G Z R H Q H Y L K Z F K I X J F
K I C I V O T U A N R A L F H K
F E R I K S E N E B K K R C Z Z
X F J D T Y K N S A L U E F I I
M A H R E Z A H S Y K L T L F T
G J K N E K N I G L I X S G V N
Q G K I V C E A H Q S D E R Y R
```

Hey, I think I spotted me in there.

In January 2018 **Harry Kane** scored his **98th** Premier League goal, which was a Spurs club record.

Striker **Alvaro Morata** became Chelsea's record signing when he joined for a cool **£60** million.

KANE

AGUERO

SALAH

LACAZETTE

MORATA

ROONEY

LUKAKU

FIRMINO

MURRAY

Eat some goals, you lot!

Leicester's **Jamie Vardy** is the first player to net against Manchester United, Manchester City, Liverpool FC, Chelsea, Spurs and Arsenal in the same Premier League season.

SON

MAHREZ

ERIKSEN

AUBAMEYANG

MARTIAL

AYEW

STERLING

ARNAUTOVIC

SANCHEZ

ANSWERS ON PAGE 61.

SPOT THE BALL

Can you work out which is the real ball in these action-packed UEFA Champions League pictures? Circle your selection now.

A round of applause if you get them all right!

Real Madrid's Isco tries to find a way past Juventus keeper Gianluigi Buffon.

1

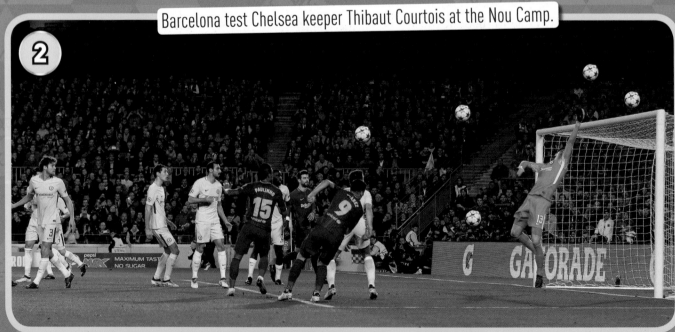

Barcelona test Chelsea keeper Thibaut Courtois at the Nou Camp.

2

3

Arjen Robben attacks for Bayern Munich against Sevilla.

4

Manchester City's Gabriel Jesus shoots past Liverpool FC.

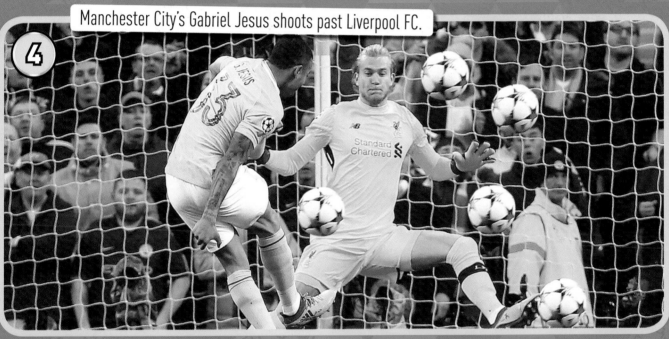

5

Sevilla go for goal at Old Trafford.

ANSWERS ON PAGE 61.

MANCHESTER MIX-UP!

Thumbs up if you spot all the changes!